ALL ABOUT
APOLO!

BY JOE LAYDEN

ALADDIN PAPERBACKS
NEW YORK LONDON TORONTO SYDNEY SINGAPORE

THIS BOOK IS DEDICATED TO ALL THE FANS
WHO HAVE SUPPORTED ME, ESPECIALLY THOSE
WHO DID BEFORE THE OLYMPIC EXPERIENCE.
YOU ALL SHARE A PIECE OF THIS WITH ME.
—APOLO ANTON OHNO

PHOTO CREDITS
FRONT COVER and BACK COVER (in bandana): Nick Vacarro.
All photos courtesy of Apolo Anton Ohno unless indicated otherwise.

First Aladdin Paperbacks edition
August 2002

Copyright © 2002
by Apolo Anton Ohno

Designed by Michael Malone

ALADDIN PAPERBACKS
An imprint of Simon & Schuster
Children's Publishing Division
1230 Avenue of the Americas
New York, NY 10020

Printed in the
United States of America
10 9 8 7 6 5 4 3 2 1

Library of Congress
Catalog Card Number 2002107417

ISBN 0-689-85610-5

Apolo Anton Ohno was right where he wanted to be . . .

"I NEVER TAKE ANY RACE FOR GRANTED . . . UNTIL I CROSS THE FINISH LINE."

—Apolo Anton Ohno

Just one turn from the finish line in the 1,000 meter final at the 2002 Winter Olympics, the world's fastest short-track speed skater was poised to strike—gold, that is. Crouching low, his fingertips gently kissing the ice with each powerful stride, Apolo made his move.

Apolo burst into the lead. The crowd at the Salt Lake Ice Center rose as one and began roaring for their countryman. This was Apolo's moment, the one he'd envisioned so many times in the previous four years.

ICON Sports Photos

Photos pp. 6-7: Phillipe Millereau/DPPI/ICON SMI

As Apolo would be the first to admit, however, nothing is certain in short-track, a frantic and sometimes dangerous sport in which skaters race in a tight circle at speeds approaching thirty-five miles per hour. As the finish line came into sight, Apolo was bumped by another skater. Suddenly there were bodies sprawled on the ice, careening out of control. Apolo crashed into the track's padded wall, felt a stabbing pain in his leg, and looked up just in time to see another skater crossing the finish line— his dream rushing away in a blur. Or so it seemed.

"I was in a daze," Apolo would later explain. "It all happened so quickly. I could feel the wind at my fingers, and the next thing I know, I'm against the boards."

But this was nothing new to Apolo. He'd been down before—lower than this, in fact. He'd known pain and disappointment on a much more personal scale, and always he had bounced back. This was just one more test.

If you think Apolo Anton Ohno, the guy with the coolest name in sports, was born into luxury and had greatness handed to him, think again. This was a kid who sometimes had a difficult

childhood, and who struggled many times before discovering and finally mastering his talent.

Apolo was born on May 22, 1982, in Seattle, Washington. His father, Yuki Ohno, was a hairdresser who had emigrated from Japan and opened his own salon. Yuki, whose father was a state university vice president, had originally studied to be an accountant. But he wanted a more interesting, artistic career. Yuki traveled a lot and worked with many famous models before settling down in the Pacific Northwest. He married a woman and the couple had a child. They named him Apolo.

A lot of people think that Apolo is named after the Greek god Apollo, but that isn't true. His first name is Greek, but it actually comes from the words "ap," meaning "steering away from," and "lo," which means "look out, here he comes." His last name, of course, is Japanese. The translation for Ohno is "great field." It's an appropriate choice for a world-class speed skater who is accustomed to leaving the competition in his wake, wouldn't you say?

Yuki didn't have a crystal ball nearby when he gave his son that name. In fact, he had no idea what to expect from Apolo, and

"I BELIEVE MY FATHER HAS [BEEN,] AND ALWAYS WILL BE, THE STRONGEST INFLUENCE IN MY LIFE. HE HAS GUIDED ME ON MANY PATHS."
— APOLO ANTON OHNO

FAMILY PHOTOS

A. A WINTER-SPORTS ENTHUSIAST—EVEN AT AGE FOUR

B. EARNING HIS NICKNAME, CHUNKIE

C. APOLO'S KINDERGARTEN PHOTO

D. Making a wish on his fifth birthday

E. Apolo and a stuffed "friend"

the challenges of raising him became even greater shortly after Apolo was born. That's when Yuki and his wife divorced, leaving Yuki to raise the boy on his own. Apolo has not seen his mother since, and has never spoken to her. He doesn't have anything bad to say about his mother, but he is quick to praise his father.

"My dad has always been there for me," Apolo says. "He's one of the hardest-working people I've ever known. I respect him in so many ways."

Not that father and son always had a cozy relationship. At times it was hard for both of them. Yuki worked long hours to keep his business afloat, and that meant Apolo spent lots of time in daycare. Sometimes he'd hang out at his dad's shop until late at night, climbing on the chairs to talk to the customers. Yuki wasn't experienced at fatherhood, but there was one thing he knew for sure: This kid had a ton of energy!

As Apolo grew, Yuki tried almost everything to keep him busy. Apolo took swimming lessons, he sang in a choir. He

YOUNG APOLO WAS A WHIRLWIND OF ENERGY—A WALKING CYCLONE IN SHORTS AND SNEAKERS.

championship. By twelve he won a state title in swimming. (His specialty was the breast stroke.) But he was getting by mostly on natural ability. Apolo trained hard when he was younger, but by junior high he became distracted by friends who didn't share the same interests. He began skipping school and spending more time with his friends than he did at home. Apolo had tons of talent, but he was in danger of throwing it all away.

Yuki worried about his son. The two began fighting. At one point Yuki threatened to send Apolo to military school if he didn't shape up. Apolo didn't listen and didn't care. On weekends he'd stay out all night with his friends. Yuki became even more concerned. He saw sports as a way to rescue his son. Yuki then thought that if Apolo dedicated himself to skating, then

even learned how to rollerskate. But there was no way to tire him out. When Yuki picked up his son at day care, the teachers would shake their heads and tell stories about how Apolo had tried to climb a fence and chew rocks. He was one of the most active kids at the center. It was also clear that Apolo was a gifted athlete. He was strong and agile, and he liked to compete. At the age of ten he won the national age group in-line skating

Apolo likes to relax by listening to rap music and R&B. He also likes to read. His all-time favorite book is *Way of the Peaceful Warrior*, a spiritual self-help book written by a former gymnast named Dan Millman.

maybe he would see how good he could be and work harder to achieve his goals. But that didn't happen. Not right away.

Apolo had become fascinated with short-track speed skating in 1994 after watching the Lillehammer Winter Olympic Games on television. To Apolo's eyes, short-track was more exciting than the traditional long-track speed skating. He liked racing against other people and not the clock. He liked the explosiveness, the speed, the way the athletes jostled for position, and the fact that it was so unpredictable. Short-track was fast, tough . . . way cool!

It helped, of course, that Apolo already knew how to skate. The first time he tried short-track, he loved it; and he worked hard to become good at it. It's a feeling he still has to this day.

"Speed skating is like floating on the ice," Apolo told *Sports Illustrated for Kids*. "When I'm in a great mood and my spirits are light, it's a beautiful feeling."

Apolo quickly became one of the top short-track speed skaters in his age group. Yuki supported his son in every way possible, even paying for ice time. He drove Apolo thousands of miles—to events as far away as Chicago and Canada—so that his son

1992 NORTHWEST USAC/RS
REGIONAL SPEED CHAMPIONSHIPS
Oaks Park, Portland, Oregon

could face the best competition. Yuki thought that success would change Apolo's attitude and help him focus on something positive. But the transformation didn't happen overnight.

Apolo got his first big break in late 1995 while competing in the United States national junior team trials. There, he was spotted by a man named Jeroen Otter, the U.S. national head team coach, who worked at the thousand miles away to live with a group of complete strangers. But the father felt he needed to have Apolo take advantage of this opportunity. In Lake Placid, Apolo would have discipline thrust upon him. He'd have access to the best coaching and training facilities in the world. Maybe there, in that sheltered world, he'd find himself.

There was just one problem: The facility had never accepted

"I WAS TOTALLY REBELLIOUS AGAINST MY DAD OR ANYONE ELSE WITH AUTHORITY."
— APOLO ANTON OHNO

Olympic Training Center in Lake Placid, New York. Apolo was young and raw, but Otter could see the boy had tremendous potential. Otter told Yuki that with time and training, Apolo could be a world-class skater.

Yuki immediately asked if it was possible for Apolo to come to Lake Placid and train under Otter—but it was one of the most difficult decisions Yuki had ever made. He was saddened by the prospect of sending his fourteen-year-old son nearly three anyone under the age of fifteen.

Otter, however, went to the U.S. Olympic Committee and argued on Apolo's behalf. He told them the kid was worth the risk, not only because he had a gift, but because he was hungry. Apolo wanted nothing more than to be the best. The committee liked the story and opened its doors to Apolo.

Unfortunately, the story wasn't entirely true, although Otter didn't know it at the time. In fact, Apolo didn't really want to move away from home, and he sure didn't like the sound of training all day. Apolo argued with his father, but Yuki's mind was made up. He drove Apolo to the airport in June of 1996, just a few weeks after the boy's fourteenth birthday, and dropped him off at the entrance. Yuki didn't know that his son had no intention of getting on the plane. Apolo waved good-bye to his father, strolled into the airport, and stopped at the first pay phone he saw.

"I called one of my older friends to pick me up at the airport and I went to his house," Apolo recalled. "I was gone for a little bit after that, and my father was pretty angry when he found out."

Eventually Apolo went back home. And a month later he found himself in Lake Placid. This time Yuki made sure Apolo got on the plane—he even went along for the ride! Before handing his son over to Otter at the training center, Yuki pulled the coach aside and wished him luck.

At first Apolo was filled with anger and resentment. A big-city kid, he hated Lake Placid, a small town nestled in the Adirondack Mountains. So he did his best to look like someone who didn't belong there, hoping perhaps he'd be sent back home. As with his life at home, he learned things from his older

friends he was training with, such as falling behind during long runs to sneak off and grab a slice of pizza and a soda.

"I hated it there," Apolo told *Sports Illustrated*. "I didn't want anybody to help me."

Apolo's outlook changed late

GETTING PERSONAL
WITH APOLO

Hair Color: brown
Eyes: hazel
Birth Weight: 6 lbs. 9 oz.
Birth Date: 5/22/82
Birth Place: Seattle, WA
Height: 5' 8"
Weight: 165 lbs.
Shoe Size: 9
Scars: upper left eyebrow, left inner thigh
Pets: cat (Tiggie)
Nicknames: chunkie, chunks, chunkles
Current Home: Colorado Springs, CO
Underwear: briefs for working out,
boxers for going out
Hobbies: cars, all kinds of sports, electronics
Collects: car magazines

What does America's fastest short-track skater have in common with Halle Berry, Hugh Jackman, Britney Spears, and Hayden Christensen? They were all included in *People* magazine's list of the 50 most beautiful people in the world. Way to go *People* magazine— now tell us something we don't know!

> The life of a world-class speed skater can be exhausting. Apolo trains as much as seven hours a day! "And people don't realize that athletes' lifestyles are not just about training," he says. "They also need the same or much more time for recovering from the workouts. Plus eating!"

that summer, when the athletes were tested to see what kind of shape they were in. Of all the speed skaters, Apolo had the highest percentage of body fat, an indication that he hadn't been working at all, and that the coaching staff was wasting its time on him. Apolo's friends had given him the nickname "Chunkie" when he was only eight years old, and now it seemed he truly deserved it.

Interestingly enough, that episode got Apolo's attention. He was embarrassed. Suddenly he felt motivated. He approached Otter and told him he wanted to improve. No—he wanted more than that. He wanted to be a champion. Otter had his doubts, but they were quickly laid to rest. Apolo began eating differently. He began winning training runs. And he skated flawlessly and furiously, like a young man on a mission.

"He totally changed," Otter says. "I'd never seen that kind of turnaround so fast."

Within a year Apolo had captured his first national

short-track championship. And he hadn't even turned fifteen yet! That performance was so impressive that a lot of people thought Apolo had a chance to win a medal at the 1998 Winter Olympics in Nagano, Japan. But his youth and inexperience, combined with a lack of proper training in the months leading up to the Olympics, were too much to overcome. He finished dead last at the Olympic Trials and failed to qualify for the U.S. team.

Apolo was so disappointed in himself that he thought about giving up speed skating. He returned to Seattle and spent a week by himself in a cottage on the coast of Washington. There was no television, no radio, no telephone, no friends. Apolo used that time to clear his head. He went for long, barefoot runs on the beach and tried to figure out what he wanted to do with his life. By the time Yuki returned to pick him up, Apolo had come to a conclusion: He decided that he wanted to get back to speed skating—and would approach the sport at 110 percent.

Over the next few years that's exactly what happened. Apolo won his first world junior title in 1999. That same year he became the youngest American ever to win a World Cup event. By 2001 Apolo had become the overall World Cup champion and a favorite to win multiple medals at the 2002 Olympics. At five feet, eight inches tall, and 165 pounds,

APOLO'S
FAVES & RAVES

Pets: Big cats **Cars:** All kinds, especially luxury cars **Food:** All Asian foods, Indian, Middle Eastern, Italian, Greek **Candy:** Don't really have a favorite, but I do like candy **Drink:** Strawberry Quik, Boba drink **Television shows:** Hmm...don't really have a television show I watch religiously **Movies:** *Rocky*, *For Love of the Game* **Actors:** Denzel Washington **Books:** Lance Armstrong's *It's Not About the Bike* and all of Dan Millman's books **Colors:** Black and red, blue and white together **Room:** the kitchen **Sports teams:** Seattle Supersonics, Colorado Avalanche **Cereal:** Cinnamon Toast Crunch, Captain Crunch with Crunch Berries **Late-night music:** R&B **Early-morning music:** Hip-hop **Athlete:** Muhammad Ali, Michael Johnson, Michael Jordan **Video game:** Street Fighter **Song:** No favorite song—they come and go **Clothes:** I love all kinds of clothes, so I can't stick to one kind **Holiday:** Christmas **Most embarrassing moment:** Getting shaving cuts while appearing on *The Tonight Show* with Jay Leno **Proudest moment:** 2002 Olympic Winter Games **Biggest regret:** Not being able to respond to all of my fans' letters and e-mails with a strong, graceful stride, he was a versatile skater who was capable of winning at every distance from 500 meters to 1,500 meters. But it wasn't just physical ability that made Apolo special.

It's been said that Apolo has a unique feel for the ice. "I feel every ripple in the ice, and I think that's something that contributes to my success," says Apolo.

There was a lot of media

the undisputed king of the rink.

Apolo had qualified for four events at Salt Lake City, but it seemed a longshot that he could win four gold medals. Short-track is simply too odd and difficult a sport for one person to dominate every event. If anyone could beat the odds, however, it was Apolo. His first race was the 1,000 meters, and it looked for a while as if he'd gotten off to a brilliant

> ## "MY QUEST, MY JOURNEY, WAS NOT ABOUT WINNING FOUR GOLD MEDALS. IT WAS ABOUT COMING TO THE OLYMPICS AND DOING MY BEST."
> — APOLO ANTON OHNO

pressure on Apolo, and he'd fought through injuries sustained from skating and even a car accident when he arrived in Salt Lake City in February of 2002. He'd been on the cover of several national magazines and had already been hailed as the biggest star of the Winter Games. He was the coolest performer in the coolest of Olympic sports. Short-track's popularity had exploded in recent years, and Apolo was

start. Apolo had strategized beautifully. He'd waited until just the right moment to seize control of the race. Then he'd surged to the front and . . .

The next thing he knew, Apolo was in the middle of a spectacular crash that dumped four of the event's five skaters onto the ice. The only person who avoided trouble was Australia's Steven Bradbury, who had been in last place. Bradbury was so far out of contention that

Phillipe Millereau/DPPI/ICON SMI

when the other skaters went down, he was able to simply glide past their fallen bodies and capture the gold medal. Apolo was stunned by the way the race unfolded, of course, but he never gave up. As Bradbury raised his arms in a display of triumph and disbelief, Apolo crawled across the finish line to take the silver medal. A few minutes later he discovered that he'd been cut by a skate when he went down. The throbbing in his upper leg was the result of a gash that would require six stitches.

Apolo hooks up with celebs Jay Leno, Christie Brinkley, and Elton John.

Though the frustrated crowd booed Bradbury's victory, Apolo was nothing but gracious despite his misfortune. He limped to the podium and accepted his silver medal with a smile. Then he shook Bradbury's hand and congratulated the winner.

"It was one of the best efforts of my life," Apolo said afterward. "I'm happy with my performance, regardless of what medal I have."

Like all great athletes, Apolo has a deep understanding of his sport. Like so many exciting sports, short-track speed skating is wildly unpredictable. That's what makes it so interesting— and so much fun to watch! Three nights later Apolo chased another medal, this time in the 1,500 meters. For a moment it looked like an instant replay. There was Apolo, crouched low, digging into the ice, preparing to make a big move as he approached the final turn. For much of the race Apolo had been near the back of the pack, but now he had passed nearly everyone. There was only one skater between him and a gold medal: South Korea's Kim Dong-Sung. As Apolo veered inside and went for the lead, Kim cut him off. Apolo immediately raised his arms to avoid a collision. Apolo's hesitation allowed Kim to cruise across the finish line in first place. Apolo took second.

Apolo suspected that Kim might be penalized for having cut him off. And the replay confirmed his belief. Moments later an announcement was made: Kim was disqualified for "cross-tracking." The judges had ruled that the Korean skater had improperly and deliberately crossed the course to interfere with another competitor. Apolo Ohno was the winner! In that instant he made history. Apolo was the first American male to win a gold medal in short-track speed skating.

As his father applauded in the stands, Apolo hugged his coaches and waved to the crowd. A broad smile creased his face. A short time later he climbed to the top step of the podium, bowed to accept his medal, and then sang along with the national anthem. For the kid who had once skipped out on training runs to wolf down pizza, it was a remarkable accomplishment. Apolo has reached his goal: He'd been there, and had given it his all.

Apolo's popularity soared in the weeks following the Winter Games. New fans were starved for information about the Olympic hero. In fact, according to the internet search engine Lycos, "Apolo Ohno" was the most requested name on the internet in the first week of March 2002. Number two was Britney Spears!

"I LOVE SHORT-TRACK. I GO OUT ON THE ICE EVERY SINGLE DAY, AND THERE'S NOT ONE DAY I DON'T WANT TO BE THERE."
— APOLO ANTON OHNO

"They can throw me in the desert and bury me," Apolo later joked. "I've got my gold medal. I'm good now."

Nothing could ever diminish what Apolo had accomplished in those first two races. Not even a disqualification in his final solo event, the 500 meters, or the failure of his United States team to win a medal in the 5,000 meters. Apolo left Salt Lake City the way he had arrived: as the brightest star of the Winter Olympics.

The next few weeks brought a whirlwind of activity: talk-show appearances, endorsement deals, and even discussions about turning his life into a movie! Pretty soon, though, it was time to get back to reality. Apolo started training again. He returned to the ice, to his second home, and the sport he loved so much. After all, most short-track speed skaters don't peak until their mid twenties. In 2006, at the next Winter Olympics, Apolo will be twenty-three years old.

So watch out world— Apolo Ohno is just getting warmed up!

"HAVE FUN AND LOVE YOUR SPORT TO THE FULLEST. HAVING FAITH IN YOURSELF AND THOSE AROUND YOU WILL HELP IN YOUR GOALS TO BECOME A GREAT ATHLETE!"